BACK TO THE BASICS

ANCHORED IN GOD

Author
OVERSEER BETTY ANDERSON

Copyright 2024 by Overseer Betty Anderson and CAE Publications - All rights reserved. It is illegal to reproduce, duplicate, or transmit any part of this document in either electronic or printed format. Recording this publication is also prohibited. References include Merriam-Webster.com, Easton's Bible Dictionary, BibleStudyTools.com, BibleHub.com, BibleGateway.com, ShiningEverBrighter.com, Wikipedia.org, bible.knowing-Jesus.com, gotquestions.org, Bible.com, New Century Bible, King James Bible, NIV Bible, Matthew Henry Commentary, and The Open Bible (Expanded Edition).

DEDICATION:

I dedicate this book to my granddaughters: Jaquitta, Brianna, and Ariel.

I acknowledge my church and church family, Jesus Is The Way of Life Ministries International. Thank you for your prayer and support.

CONTENTS

BABES	*1*
GOD	*8*
JESUS – YESHUA	*14*
THE HOLY SPIRIT	*23*
GRACE	*32*
MERCY	*44*
GLORY	*53*
TRUTH	*63*
POWER	*73*
FAITH	*81*
FORGIVENESS	*92*
SALVATION	*102*

INTRODUCTION:

This book, **Back to the Basics**, serves as a blueprint for how God created us to take our Kingdom position with Him. It acts as both an introduction for some readers and a review for others. The basics will never be obsolete; they are eternal. When we hold fast to the basics outlined in this book, we become committed disciples of Christ. We are encouraged to remember that:

1. God's Word is true.
2. Truth has a name: Jesus.
3. We are disciples, or followers, of Jesus.
4. Anchored in God and cannot be moved.
5. The adversary, the devil, is defeated.

Back to the Basics provides nourishment for spiritual growth. While this book is not the Bible, it can be a useful companion for study. We must remember to study. Second Timothy 2:15 says, "Study to show thyself approved unto God, a workman that needs not to be ashamed, rightly dividing the word of truth." We will not do better until we know better.

We all want to grow. In order to mature as disciples and ambassadors of Christ, we cannot remain like babies. We need to grow up to full stature. Just as Jesus was born in the same way we are physically, spiritually, He was God. The Father wanted Jesus to demonstrate life for us, allowing Him to experience our existence. So, Jesus grew, and we must grow too.

To grow means to build, develop, expand, produce, flourish, advance, mature, abound, rise, age, and increase. It signifies becoming more advanced or developed. Returning to and reviewing the basics enhances, improves, and increases our spiritual growth.

Without the basics, our spiritual lives can become stunted. When we neglect them, our growth in the Word declines, and we lose connection with what we need for spiritual development. The basics anchor us. We hold onto God's unchanging hand and grow up!

I hope you dive deeper into the study of God's word. This book is meant to be a companion guide. God bless us all!

Chapter One

BABES

2 Peter 3:18: "But grow in the grace and knowledge of our Lord and Savior, Jesus Christ. To Him be glory both now and forever! Amen."

Babes do not have the strength, stamina, or power that grown-ups do. They cannot rule or command; they learn through trial and error. Babes can be easily deceived by craftiness, beauty, and stimulation. They are often dominated by their flesh, feelings, and outward distractions. I like to call it the "I need, I feel, I want" syndrome. To me, that is the baby test. And let us not forget the tantrum that follows when they do not get their way: "If I do not get my way!"

There is no place in the kingdom of God for such behavior. Babes are led by their appetites, and they resist discipline. They do not embrace training, rules, or codes of conduct. They want what they want, when they want it, and how they want it. That is how you can spot them.

1 Corinthians 3:1-2 says, "And I, brethren, could not speak unto you as unto spiritual, but as unto carnal, even as unto babes in Christ. I have fed you with milk and not with meat; for hitherto you were not able to bear it, neither yet now are you able."

This is a spiritual matter, and we must not get it twisted. Our flesh is weak. We should not focus on outward appearances or rely solely on our natural senses. As grown-ups and believers, we need solid food to continue growing and maturing.

As kingdom-grown-ups, we can:

1. Live with moral integrity.
2. Study God's word and apply it to our lives.
3. Listen to and obey the Holy Spirit.
4. Love the truth, even when it hurts.
5. Fast and pray.
6. Know our kingdom assignment and fulfill it.
7. Be disciplined, not despising correction.

Each of us in the body of Christ has an assignment, and it is time to step into that role!

Babes cannot follow through on assignments. As grown-ups, we: 1. Study, learn, and grow; 2. Develop a lifestyle of fasting and praying; 3. Keep our eyes on Jesus; 4. Desire correction.

Babies despise correction. At times, it seems like they take correction as an invitation to continue their unacceptable behavior. Then, when something bad happens, they throw fits and tantrums.

The Word of God has much to say to us, but some are "dull of hearing." Hebrews 5:11-14 states, "Of whom we have many things to say and hard to be uttered, seeing you are dull of hearing. For when for the time you ought to be teachers, you have need that one teach you again, which be the first principles of the oracles of God. You have become such as have need of milk and not of strong meat. For everyone that uses milk is unskillful in the word of righteousness; for he is a babe. But strong meat belongs to them that are of full age, even those who, by reason of use, have their senses exercised to discern both good and evil."

Many times, we resist sound doctrine because we do not understand.

Having dull understanding and dull hearing can lead us astray and leave us vulnerable to deception.

Dull hearing means not comprehending with full knowledge or understanding. That is baby-like behavior.

Dull hearing can go away through study, prayer, and fasting. Without these, we remain in a state of ignorance and immaturity. Simply put, we do not know. We need to experience things to learn and to know. Babies do not know through experience yet, so they end up doing the same things repeatedly. We all have our "I do not know" moments. In those cases, we are ignorant. But being ignorant is not sinful. What is sinful is not growing and learning. We must grow both naturally and spiritually. God created us with growth potential and a desire to know Him.

To know or to understand carries with it corresponding behavior. I like to say, when we know better, we do better. The Word of God teaches us, but often we refuse to listen and obey because we are dull of hearing. We go along, thinking all is well, when we are actually out of order. Babies often think they are always right.

Babies need correction. Left to their own ways, they create dysfunction, disorder, and confusion. Disorder, chaos, and confusion might be fine with babes, but they should not be found in the body of Christ. For babies, ignorance is bliss.

Bliss means perfect happiness, great joy, contentment, harmony, jubilation, and mirth. Ignorance can lead us to think we can find bliss in the world. However, believers who know God's Word understand that true bliss comes only from obedience to God and His Word. God is the only source of perfect joy, peace, and happiness.

Spiritual grown-ups in the Word of God know the source of bliss: it comes from heaven through the Lord Jesus Christ. Babies do not comprehend this. Instead, they indulge in earthly pleasures, mistaking them for bliss. They enjoy temporary sensations and soon find themselves longing for more. Earthly pleasures can become lifelong pursuits for them.

Babies cannot break free from themselves. Sadly, too many believers are still searching for gratification and satisfaction of desires. Grown-ups, on the other hand, seek to please Christ.

Spiritual grown-ups in Christ know what bliss is!

1. They are raised up with Christ; 2. The joy of the Lord is their strength; 3. They are seated with Christ in heavenly places now; 4. They have power over the enemy and all evil works; 5. The Word of God is their weapon; 6. They can do all things through Christ who strengthens them; 7. All their enemies are defeated; 8. All needs are met; 9. Their words bless; 10. Their words can curse; 11. Love fulfills the law; 12. Whoever does not love does not know God.

That is my partial list of what Kingdom bliss means to me. Now, compile your own list and add to mine what you know is bliss. We know ignorance is not bliss, and we recognize that babies often cling to ignorance.

Our enemy, Satan, is strong, relentless, full of envy, wrath, and fierceness. Babies are not skillful warriors. So, we must grow up in Christ. We need to reach full stature. Our God silences the enemy and puts our foes to shame. Babies are not adept at putting on and using the weapons of warfare. In the Kingdom of God, babies are meant to grow into mature believers; they need to put on their armor and fight the enemies instead of each other.

Our God tells us to fight the good fight of faith. As it says in 1 Timothy 6:12, "Fight the good fight of faith, lay hold of eternal life, whereunto you are also called and have professed a good profession before many witnesses."

The world is watching and judging. They eagerly await believers' failures because they recognize baby behavior. Let us grow up before many witnesses. They are watching.

Chapter Two

GOD

Genesis 1:1: "In the beginning, God..."

This author will not attempt to prove, through debate, that God exists. That is a personal decision. Either you believe in a supreme, all-seeing, all-knowing, all-powerful God, or you do not. Personally, I believe in the God of the Bible. The Oxford Dictionary defines God as a superhuman being or spirit worshipped as having power over nature and all human fortunes. Many other sources offer names and descriptions of gods or deities, and there are also goddesses described as powerful supernatural beings.

These pages are not intended for a debate about God; instead, the focus is on the God of Christianity. God is eternal and supreme, the creator and preserver of all. He is one—He cannot be referred to as "they." He is spiritual, not natural, and should never be called "it." He is not of nature; He created and designed it. He is invisible, the creator who controls all of creation. God is the creator, the sustainer, and the ruler of the universe.

As creator, He brought everything into existence—everything, not just some things—using nothing but what He Himself made. As sustainer, He holds everything together, whether seen or unseen. As ruler, He controls and commands all things. Everything—no exceptions—is subject to Him!

God is omniscient. He knows all. He knows everything from the beginning to the end, including our lives. He knows our rising and our sitting down. He sees the rising of the sun and its setting.

God is omnipresent. He is always present. There is nowhere to go from His presence. Psalm 139:7 asks, "Where can I go from your spirit?" The psalmist goes on to say that our God is present on earth and in heaven. In darkness and in light, on the mountains and in the valleys, even babies are not hidden in their mother's womb. How marvelous is that? He is there for good and not for evil.

God is omnipotent. He is all-powerful. There is nothing outside of His reach. He can do all things. Think rationally for a moment: why would someone worship a statue, a tree, a river, or anything else made—even a person? Those "things" can do nothing. God asks us, "Who can do the things that I do?" It is a personal question. What is your answer?

Deuteronomy 4:35 states, "To you, it is shown that you might know that the Lord, He is God; there is no other besides Him." Nehemiah 9:6 adds, "You alone are the Lord. You have made the heavens, the heaven of heavens with all their hosts, the earth and all that is in it, the seas and all that is in them; you give life to all of them. And the heavenly host bows down before you."

God is God! God is Lord! Jesus is God! Jesus is Lord! There is no confusion here; there is no double talk. Jesus is God in human form. God, who can do anything, made Himself a body—Jesus. This just emphasizes the power of God. Just as He made man from the dirt of the ground, He, with His power, divided Himself, made a body like ours for Himself, impregnated a chosen vessel, and came into the earth. It was a miraculous pregnancy. Jesus is the image of the invisible God. God sent Jesus at the perfect time. God showed Himself "man to man." This is how we know that He is God!

Galatians 4:4-5 states, "But when the fullness of time was come, God sent forth His Son, made of a woman, made under the law to redeem them that were under the law, that we might receive the adoption of sons."

This is how we become sons of God. We believe that God did this. God becomes our Father because Jesus is our Savior. God gave Jesus the kingdom. Jesus Christ is Lord. He is the same Lord as the Father. Now we see just how powerful our God is. He made Himself a body, came to earth as a man, but lived as God, demonstrating the power of God on earth.

Acts 16:31 says, "And they said, believe on the Lord Jesus Christ, and thou shalt be saved." One might ask: why does not God just save everybody? What do we need to be saved from? What is the danger? God wants volunteers. He desires those who make deliberate decisions to follow Him—not robots, not AI.

If God had wanted blind, commanded worship, He could have set it that way, but He gave us choice. Thank God! We can do what we want, when we want, how we want, and with whom we want. He gives us the choice to believe or not to believe. It is wonderful! We are thinking beings, and when we recognize that there is a choice to be made, we can make that choice.

He told us to choose whom we would serve. He says, "If I am God, serve Me." He also says, "If you believe there is some other god, serve it."

That is love, no pressure, no restraints, just choice. God says, "I love you, and I want you to love me. Choose to love me." John 3:16 reminds us: "For God so loved the world that He gave His only begotten Son, that whosoever believes in Him will not perish but will have everlasting life."

God's greatest identity, description, and representation is love. Everything we see—and even what we cannot see—is a product of God's love. When we look in the mirror, we see God's love. When we gaze at trees, grass, rivers, and all the wonders of nature, it is God's love. The air we breathe is God's love. Our bodies, organs, the blood in our veins—each is a testament to God's love. God loved the world so much that He sent Jesus as our Savior. He showed divine love when He gave Himself for us.

This is how we know we belong to God: through our love for Him and for each other. Love is an action word. The only way to truly understand it is through demonstration. For God so loved that He gave—That is action. He created the world (action), He loved (action), He saved (action).

It is one thing to say, "I love you," but it is even greater to show it. Everlasting life is the beautiful benefit we gain from this love we share for God and one another.

In John 13:34, Jesus tells us, "I give you a new commandment: love one another." God is love, as stated in 1 John 4:7-21.

Here are some key points:

1. Love is born of God and knows God.
2. If we love one another, God abides in us, and His love is perfected in us.
3. God is love, and whoever abides in love abides in God, and God in him.
4. Perfect love casts out fear.
5. We love others because God loves us.
6. If I hate my brother whom I have seen, how can I love God whom I have not seen?
7. Whosoever loves God must also love his brother.

Father, thank You for Your power, Your presence, and for knowing all things. Thank You for Jesus, my Savior. Thank You for loving me and giving me the power to love others. In the name of Jesus, amen.

Chapter Three

JESUS – YESHUA

GOD IS OUR SALVATION

Matthew 1:19-25: "Then Joseph, her husband, being a just man and not willing to make her a public example, was minded to put her away privately. But while he thought on these things, behold, the angel of the Lord appeared unto him in a dream, saying, 'Joseph, thou son of David, fear not to take unto thee Mary thy wife. For that which is conceived in her is of the Holy Ghost. And she shall bring forth a son, and thou shalt call his name Jesus, for he shall save his people from their sins.' Now all this was done that it might be fulfilled which was spoken of the Lord by the prophet, saying, 'Behold, a virgin shall be with child and shall bring forth a son, and they shall call his name Immanuel,' which being interpreted is God with us. Then Joseph, being raised from sleep, did as the angel of the Lord had bidden him and took unto him his wife, and knew her not till she had brought forth her firstborn son, and he called his name Jesus."

Acts 2:21: "And it shall come to pass that whosoever shall call upon the name of the Lord shall be saved."

There is a personal question for each of us, and the answer is equally personal: Who is Jesus? As you can see above, He has many names. To this day, He remains the most debated person in all of history. Everything revolves around Him. Once, while on earth, He asked His followers, "Who do you say that I am?" Check that out in Matthew 16:13-16, Mark 8:27-29, and Luke 9:18-20. He asked because He wanted to know if they believed He was our Lord. We cannot go halfway. Either He is the second person of the Godhead, or He is not. This revelation is based on each person's faith. Either you believe He is God, or you do not.

Each person must decide what to do with Jesus. His name says it all, but we must believe He is the Savior of men. There is the matter of sin, iniquity, and transgression. Man is guilty of it all, so we need a Savior. We cannot save ourselves. That is not possible; trying would be like bathing in the same bathwater over and over again. To be cleansed, we need a Savior who is clean and pure of all sin. Only God is clean. Because of His mercy and grace, God sent His Son, Jesus.

Jesus took upon Himself the sins of the whole world—your sins, my sins, and everyone else's. All who believe in Him will not perish. He can do it because He is without sin.

I call Him Jesus. You can choose your own name of endearment. Personalize your love language. By faith, we build our own personalized relationship with Jesus. We develop our relationship with Him after the first step of believing that He is infinite, eternal, unchangeable, wise, powerful, holy, just, good, and true. He is all God. The Father made for Himself a body and came into the earthly realm as man. He did this to give us hope and a future of good.

Colossians 1:15-21 (NIV): "The Son is the image of the invisible God, the firstborn over all creation. For in Him all things were created: things in heaven and on earth, visible and invisible."

Because God is all-powerful, He can do what is impossible for anything or anyone else. God created man in His own image, using one who is just like Him to save and deliver all others. Man, through Adam, tainted God's image.

In the beginning, through Adam, man became an unholy, ungodly image. God sent Jesus to show what a godly image looks like and how it acts.

An image is an outline of an original. "Image" means likeness or similarity. So God created man like Himself, but man polluted himself. We see that man separated himself from God. Man changed the divine DNA that God placed within him and became sinful flesh and blood. Because of that, men needed a Savior to put them in right standing with God. This Savior is Jesus. He alone is the image of God. He is the true quality. He embodies the complete character of God. Jesus alone reveals God's personality, deeds, thoughts, words, and appearance. Jesus is God.

God gave Himself a body, a body in the likeness of sinful men, so that He could bring men back to Himself. He restored man to where he was before sin entered into him. Jesus had to be like man, but without sin, so He could save men. Only God could do that.

Hebrews 2:16-18: "For verily, He took not on Himself the nature of angels, but He took on Him the seed of Abraham. Wherefore, in all things, it behooved Him to be made like unto His brethren, that He might be a merciful and faithful high priest in things pertaining to God, to make reconciliation for the sins of the people.

For in that He Himself had suffered being tempted, He is able to succor them that are tempted."

You see, the man that sins shall die. To die means to be separated from God. That is why we live in Him. Like Him, we live.

We escape spiritual death through the shed blood of Jesus. While physical death still occurs, it serves to cast off the flesh and usher in the new eternal life for all who believe. The people who crucified Jesus could not grasp this profound truth; they hated Him. He came as a man, acted like God, died on the cross as prophesied, rose from the dead, and ascended back to the Father in heaven—all while proclaiming His equality with God.

John 5:23 states, "That all men should honor the Son even as they honor the Father. He that honors not the Son honors not the Father, which has sent Him."

In John 5:18, we read, "Therefore, the Jews sought to kill Him because He not only had broken the Sabbath but said also that God was His Father, making Himself equal with God."

To be equal means to be uniform, matching, the same in size, degree, and identity, as well as having the ability to meet the challenge. Jesus fits this description perfectly and is indeed one with God. He and the Father are one!

One significant hurdle for many unbelievers is looking beyond Jesus as merely a man. For some, it is hard to fathom that a person born of a woman could be the God of all creation. Yet, He is! All who receive Him must believe that He is who He says He is.

Hebrews 11:6 reminds us, "But without faith, it is impossible to please Him, for he that comes to God must believe that He is and that He is a rewarder of them that diligently seek Him." The reward is a new life through Jesus Christ, available to all who believe. The old life is gone, replaced by a new, eternal life through Christ Jesus our Lord.

Jesus being born in human form—His shape, structure, and nature—throws many people off. Many struggle to see beyond His physical existence. They point to His birth from a man and woman, His childhood, His need for food and sleep, His death on the cross, His refusal to save Himself, and His literal bleeding to death. In the eyes of many, God wouldn't subject Himself to such experiences, but He did! It was His way of restoring humanity back to Himself, back to the Creator.

Acts 4:12 declares, "Neither is there salvation in any other: for there is none other name under heaven given among men, whereby we must be saved."

Jesus is called the Messiah because He came into the world to save sinners—just like us. Being saved means being taken out of danger and destruction. He is the only one who can accomplish this. God's plan is for us to spend eternity with Him, and we can only be presentable to Him through Jesus' cleansing blood. That is why He went to the cross; it had to be done.

This is the will of God. Only Jesus is our salvation, our Messiah, our Savior. Many impostors will come, but the Spirit of the Lord helps us discern the truth from the fake.

Romans 10:13 tells us, "For whosoever shall call upon the name of the Lord shall be saved." And the name of the Lord is JESUS!

John 3:16 beautifully states, "For God so loved the world that He gave His one and only Son, that whosoever believes in Him shall not perish but have eternal life."

Let us personalize it: "For I call upon the name of the Lord, and I am saved. For God loves me so much that He gave Jesus, His only Son, for me. I believe in Him, so I will not perish, but I have eternal life. AMEN."

1 Corinthians 15:20-22 says, "But now is Christ risen from the dead and become the first fruits of them that slept. For since by man came death, by man came also the resurrection of the dead. For as in Adam all die, even so, in Christ shall all be made alive."

Let these truths sink in and transform your heart!

Jesus, the Christ, was crucified, buried, and rose on the third day. He is the Anointed One, the only begotten of the Father. God poured all of Himself—His power, glory, grace, and eternity—into Jesus Christ.

Jesus holds all the power of God. And just to clarify, "Christ" is not His last name; it represents His Spirit and is closely associated with His resurrection from the dead. If He hadn't risen, there would be no salvation from sin, no chance for eternal life with Him. These are just a few of the incredible benefits of serving Jesus Christ, the Messiah, our Savior.

In the Bible, Jesus describes Himself in John 4:25-26. Here, He's having a conversation with a woman at a well, and He reveals Himself by using the name of God: "I Am." He calls Himself Christos, Messiah, Savior, and the Anointed One. When we receive Him, He becomes our Father in heaven. All we need to do is believe on the Lord Jesus Christ, and we will be saved.

Father God, I believe that Jesus was born of a virgin, died on the cross, rose from the dead, ascended to heaven, and has cleansed me from all unrighteousness. I receive eternal life in Jesus' name. Amen.

Chapter Four

HOLY SPIRIT, HOLINESS AND PRAYER

1 John 5:7-8: "For there are three that bear record in heaven: the Father, the Word, and the Holy Spirit, and these three are one."

Matthew 28:19: "Go ye therefore and teach all nations, baptizing them in the name of the Father, and of the Son, and of the Holy Ghost."

2 Corinthians 13:14: "The grace of our Lord Jesus Christ, the love of God, and the communion of the Holy Ghost be with you all. Amen."

There is so much debate about God. Is He real? Does He really have an effect on what man does? How can we prove that He exists? So many questions, so much discussion. Personally, I do not engage in debates about the God I serve. I have a belief, I have an understanding, and I do not argue about it. What I know, I know!

This is how I see it: God is one. He is composed of three persons. He does not have a split personality.

He is one. Look at it this way: you are one person, just one person, but you can present yourself in several ways. Perhaps you are a parent, a sibling, an aunt, or an uncle. You are all of these roles at the same time. You are still just one person. See God as having three roles: Father, Son, and Holy Spirit—all at the same time.

Our Father sent Jesus to show us who He is. He is all-powerful, the chief potentate, all-knowing, and full of love. Believers call Him Lord God Almighty. Jesus is our Savior, Deliverer, Healer, Advocate, and Power. He is the God-man. We call Him Lord Jesus.

The Holy Spirit is the revealer. He teaches us all things pertaining to life and godliness. He is the indwelling Lord. He is our guide into who and what God wants us to be. He is our Comforter. He works from the inside of the believer. The Holy Spirit is a person; we never call Him "it."

John 14:26: "But the Comforter, which is the Holy Ghost, whom the Father will send in my name, He shall teach you all things, and bring all things to your remembrance, whatsoever I have said unto you." Jesus was saying that He was going away, but the Father would send someone to help, someone to comfort them.

The Holy Spirit teaches the ways of God and also brings the Word of God to our remembrance. The Holy Spirit works from the inside out. As a person, the Holy Spirit comforts and shows compassion for others. He reveals or explains things to believers. The Holy Spirit conforms us into what our God wants us to be. Holy Spirit-filled believers are not ignorant of worldly or spiritual matters because the Holy Spirit reveals.

There cannot be too much emphasis on God's Holy Spirit. Believers need to always recognize Him, at all times. We cannot see Him, but He makes His presence known to believers. Jesus went back to be with the Father, and the Father sent His Holy Spirit to lead and guide us through our earthly lives.

Sadly, today, so much emphasis is put on dancing, clapping, shouting, speaking in tongues, and other outward expressions as signs of the Holy Spirit is presence. All of that is great, but what God says is that we shall receive power after the Holy Spirit comes upon us and dwells in us. We need power to live holy.

The world today is full of lies, deceit, deception, and evil. Without God's Holy Spirit, we cannot discern between the things of God and the things of the devil.

The only way to know the truth is through the indwelling Holy Spirit. That is what Jesus said in John 14:6: "I am the way, the truth, and the life." The Holy Spirit is God with us and God in us. Everything is subject to the Father's will. Jesus shows us who God is, while the Holy Spirit teaches us who we are in God.

John 14:25-26: "But the Advocate, the Holy Spirit, whom the Father will send in my name, will teach you all things and will remind you of everything I have said to you." Only you, for yourself, can know for sure that God Himself has come to live in you. God dwells in us when we receive Jesus as our Lord and Savior. The Holy Spirit translates us out of the kingdom of darkness into the kingdom of light. The Holy Spirit changes these earthen vessels into temples of God.

1 Corinthians 6:19: "Know ye not that your body is the temple of the Holy Spirit, which is in you, whom you have of God, and ye are not your own?" By this, we know that the Holy Spirit dwells in us: 1) that we love the Lord with our whole heart, 2) that we love others as we love ourselves, and 3) that we live in holiness.

HOLINESS

1 Peter 1:15-16: "But as He who called you is holy, you also be holy in all your conduct, because it is written, 'Be holy, for I am holy.'" Holy means being set aside for a particular use. In this sense, for us, it means that we live a life for God. Everything we think or do comes under His standards when we are saved. That means when we give our lives to God, we become His; we become saints; we become His possession. We live for Him, by Him, and through Him. We only want to please Him. We only want to live lives acceptable to Him.

God, our Father, paid a priceless price for us when He sent Jesus. We want to show our love and appreciation for our Savior by living lives that are acceptable to Him. We do not want to embarrass Him. The blood of Jesus sanctifies us, which means it cleanses us and removes all the dirt and stains that sin has caused.

Jesus has made us holy, sanctified, righteous, and perfect by dying and shedding His blood to take away our sin. Hebrews 10:14 says, "For by one sacrifice He has made perfect forever those who are being made holy."

The word "perfect" means complete, whole, immovable, and abounding. That is what the Holy Spirit does for the believer.

The Holy Spirit has a voice. He is a person who guides us to holiness, and we must learn to hear His voice. He speaks to us often, primarily through His Word. The written Word, or the Bible, expresses our God. The Holy Spirit teaches us how to obey the Word of God, who is Jesus. The more we desire Him, the more we receive of Him. He is free to all who believe.

If we want to know Him, He is available. He is ever-present. Some of us have become experts at ignoring Him. I've found that He knows how to get our attention, and it is not always a still, small voice—though often it is. But sometimes, He chastises us as a wake-up call. It might not feel good, but He works all things for our good. Even if it feels like a spanking from the Holy Spirit, it is for our benefit. He is working out a purpose in us, making us into what He created us to be. Romans 8:28 reminds us, "And we know that in all things, God works for the good of those who love Him, who have been called according to His purpose."

The Holy Spirit tells us what God wants, and we want what God wants. That fulfills our purpose.

Our reason for being is to live a righteous, holy life to glorify God, and His Holy Spirit helps us achieve that.

PRAYER

Romans 8:26-28 says, "The Spirit helps us in our weakness. We do not know how to pray as we should. But the Spirit Himself speaks to God for us, even begs God for us with deep feelings that words cannot explain." God can see what is in people's hearts and helps us at all times. Our thoughts and emotions can often be all over the place. Not only do we not know how to pray, but we also often do not know what to pray for. Thank God that He knows everything! It is such a relief to know that our God is not far away. He knows we need help to become who He wants us to be. He understands that we are often crisis believers—only praying when there is stress, distress, problems, or calamities. Because the Holy Spirit is patient and kind, He will pray for us and teach us to pray.

Sometimes, we do not have to say a word; His Spirit speaks for us. This is perfect for us because He knows exactly what we need. He promises to give us what we need.

Often, our hearts are so broken, and the weight of life is so heavy that we do not have the words. In those moments, we weep and call out to our God, and That is okay. The Holy Spirit is patient and kind. He does not get tired of us; He wants us to persist—not because He is hard of hearing or punishing us, but because He wants us to keep the faith. Ephesians 6:18 encourages us to "...pray at all times in the Spirit, and stay alert in this with perseverance and intercession for all the saints." We pray for ourselves and for others.

The Holy Spirit will also help us study the Word of God so that we will know what and how to pray. Each of us will communicate with God differently, but we should all pray in agreement with God's Word. Studying and memorizing Scripture is important for powerful prayers. Many people rely on scripted, printed, published prayers. These are fine for beginners, new believers, and moments of reflection. However, we should speak to God from the depths of our own hearts. If we ask the Holy Spirit, He will teach us to pray. Discover for yourself the peace and power that comes from your prayers. A good suggestion is to start by having a simple conversation with the Holy Spirit. This will build a verbal relationship, allowing you to listen to Him and get to know His voice, which will strengthen your relationship with God.

Luke 18:1 states, "And He spoke a parable to them to this end, that men ought always to pray and not to faint." Always means always. It means do not stop. Do not take a break or a breather. It means to be persistent, to keep going again and again, never giving up. That is how we keep from fainting. Fainting means being tired, worn out, and unable to go on—too weak.

Remember to pray sincerely and privately, not for show. Listen to yourself and ask the Holy Spirit for help. Avoid using vain, empty, repetitive words and phrases. Practice and memorize the prayer Jesus taught in Matthew Chapter 6. We cannot go wrong praying The Word.

Father, thank You for Your Holy Spirit. Thank You for working out Your purpose in my life, for giving me the power to live holy, and for teaching me how to pray without ceasing. Amen.

Chapter Five

GRACE

Ephesians 2:8-9
"For by grace are ye saved through faith, and that not of yourselves; it is the gift of God, not of works, lest any man should boast."

Grace is God's power to save and deliver. Only God can rescue us from eternal destruction. Why does He do it? Because He loves us and knows that we cannot save ourselves.

We do not deserve grace, but He gives us grace upon grace—multiplied grace. To be saved means to be kept from danger and destruction. Destruction was our destiny until Jesus died on the cross. That is grace—He did what no one else would do for the undeserving.

2 Corinthians 12:9 "My grace is sufficient for you, for my power is made perfect in weakness." You see, beloved, grace is power. It took God's power for Jesus to hang on the cross. He didn't have to do it, but He did, and that is grace.

God's grace is enough for all who believe. We do not need anything else. Nothing else can provide for us eternally. He is sufficient. That means He is qualified, competent, complete, and adequate to save. When Jesus hung on the cross, He could do it because the Father sent Him. He had to have the power, or grace, of God to carry it out. It was a demonstration of love that was utterly undeserved. Surely, we did not deserve Jesus's sacrifice.

Jesus had the grace, or power, of the Father to suffer and die. Matthew 26:39 "My Father, if it be possible, let this cup pass away from me; nevertheless, not my will, but as you will." Jesus was relying on God's grace—His power working in Him. He needed His Father's grace to bring Him through, just as we need God's grace to bring us through.

It takes a personal revelation. Knowing grace is personal. Grace is God's power in us to be who He wants us to be. It is free—a gift with no charge. You can have a gift and not know it, or you can choose to ignore it. For example, because of God's grace, Jesus came to take away our sin. But if we do not believe or receive this grace, we will not benefit from His free gift.

We cannot do anything to deserve this gift of grace. In the Old Testament, the law was given by the grace of God. Without the law, all would have perished. The law provided guidance on how God commanded them to live. The law was given under grace.

When we look at the law, we sometimes think of it as hard to keep. We forget to see it through the eyes of a gracious God. But we understand today that God took it to another level in Jesus. The law was God's saving grace in the old way. It established God's way so that people wouldn't be lost and separated from Him.

Grace and truth have been fulfilled in the Lord Jesus Christ. In Jesus, God has shown Himself to be gracious to all who believe. God's grace covers the law with the blood of Jesus. Grace transformed the law into love—no longer focusing on the offense but on Jesus's sacrifice.

Grace is present in both the Old and New Testaments. It is through the Lord Jesus Christ that grace and truth were fully revealed. As John 1:17 tells us, "For the law was given by Moses, but grace and truth came by Jesus Christ." Jesus shed His blood to pay the sin debt we owed. He did not abolish the law of God; instead, He fulfilled it.

He took away the sting of death for all who believe and receive His grace. In doing so, Jesus satisfied the death penalty; we do not face eternal death because He took that death upon Himself. That, my friends, is God's grace.

Our understanding of grace deepens as we continually study, pray, and yield to the Holy Spirit. As 2 Peter 3:18 reminds us, "But grow in grace and in the knowledge of our Lord and Savior Jesus Christ." We live out grace as we grow in our knowledge of Christ and obey Him. He empowers us to lead holy lives. Growth may be gradual, but it is sure. Just like we transition from infants to adults, we mature in grace. We nourish ourselves with the Word of God, immersing ourselves in it daily. Grace is the power of God that sustains us.

Despite our unworthiness, God's love remains unwavering. He sees beyond our faults and forgives us. In turn, we must extend grace to others, even when they may not seem deserving of our kindness. The ability to be gracious comes from God. Philippians 2:13 says, "For it is God who works in us both to will and to do His good pleasure." We are here to please God, not to seek the approval of ourselves or others.

Because of the grace in our lives, we can help heal broken hearts, bear others' burdens, and bind up wounds. God's grace empowers us to give grace. The grace we receive freely, we are called to give freely. As Matthew 10:7-8 instructs, we are to proclaim that the kingdom of heaven is at hand. We should heal the sick, cleanse the lepers, raise the dead, and cast out demons; "freely we have received, so freely we give." By God's grace, we can love the "unlovable" because, without His grace, we would be just like them.

Here are some practical ways to extend grace to others, but remember, we need God's power working in us to do these things:

1. Choose Your Words Wisely

Carefully check your words to avoid causing heartbreak, hurt, misunderstanding, conflict, and severe consequences. Spirit-filled, gracious words uplift the listener. Colossians 4:6 encourages us, "Let your speech always be gracious, seasoned with salt, so that you may know how you ought to answer each person."

We must ensure that the words we speak, and the meditations of our hearts are acceptable to God as the Holy Spirit works within us.

Grace acts as a seasoning that can bring life to those who hear it. Remember, the tongue can bring either life or death; it is a powerful weapon.

Proverbs 18:21 reminds us that life and death are in the power of the tongue. By the grace of God, may we use our words to share Christ with a world that desperately needs Him.

So let us embrace grace, not only for ourselves but also as a gift to those around us.

2. Find Ways to Help Others

Look for ways to lend a hand whenever you can. Seek opportunities to be helpful without any prejudice or discrimination. As Hebrews 13:16 reminds us, "Do not neglect to do good and to share what you have, for such sacrifices are pleasing to God."

Let us not live in fear of not having enough. There will always be people in need of food, clothes, shelter, a kind word, some understanding, or someone to mourn with or celebrate with. We need to resist being stingy or judgmental, which often holds us back from helping others. Sometimes, we fear that we will not have enough for ourselves.

But as Proverbs 19:17 says, "Those who are gracious toward the poor lend to the Lord, and the Lord will fully repay them." This means our gracious God gives back to us with interest. He helps us as we help others.

3. Release Grudges and Offenses

Ephesians 4:31-32 tells us, "Get rid of bitterness, rage, anger, brawling, slander, malice, and violence. Be kind to one another, forgiving one another just as Christ forgave us." And that is only possible by His grace! We show God's grace when we live in love, peace, and unity.

It takes God's grace for us to love those we might consider unlovable. 1 John 4:7 states, "Beloved, let us love one another, for love is of God, and everyone who loves is born of God and knows God." This is the real test—the measuring stick for those who say they love God. We can only pass this test by the grace (and power) of God.

Holding onto grudges and offenses makes it nearly impossible to walk in love. God does not hold grudges or offenses against us. By grace, the blood of Jesus presents us as blameless. Through the Holy Spirit, we must do the same for others.

Offense is serious. Offenses will come. An offense is a resentment caused by a perceived insult and can be a disregard for personal standards or principles. It is something that hurts our ego. The natural response is often revenge. Some of us hold on to offenses for years, even if the person who hurt us is long gone. But we need to let the grace of God rule our hearts. We might think that the offender does not deserve our kindness or forgiveness, but we must remember Jesus. He forgave us through His loving kindness and grace, allowing us to overcome those offenses.

Ephesians 4:32 encourages us to "be kind to one another, tenderhearted, forgiving one another, even as God for Christ's sake has forgiven you." We were unlovable, yet by grace, God redeemed us. We offended Him with our sin and disobedience, and He redeemed us through the blood of Jesus. He is gracious to us. Everyone who loves has been born of God and knows God; those who do not love do not know God because God is love. This is serious, but by the grace of God and His power working in us, we can let go of grudges, offenses, and any negative feelings or thoughts we have toward others.

4. Be Thankful at All Times

1 Thessalonians 5:18 says, "Rejoice always, pray continually, give thanks in all circumstances; for this is the will of God for you in Christ Jesus." We are called to rejoice all the time and to be glad. The will of God is for us to be thankful at all times, and achieving that takes the grace of God.

Throughout the Word, God urges His people to give thanks. In Psalm 100:4-5, it says, "Enter into His gates with thanksgiving and into His courts with praise. Be thankful unto Him and bless His name, for the Lord is good. His mercy is everlasting, and His truth endures to all generations." Because of His grace, we can enter into His presence. When we do, our hearts overflow with gratitude. Our praise is a reflection of our appreciation for all He has done.

We thank Him for His grace, mercy, longsuffering, life, health, strength, and salvation. We thank Him for everything. He is so gracious, and we are so thankful.

It is because of His grace that we are not consumed or utterly destroyed. Jesus modeled a life of thanksgiving and gratitude.

He knew His Father was with Him at all times, and the same goes for us. Because the Father is always with us, we can remain grateful in all circumstances.

Adverse situations do not diminish God's grace. What is happening around us does not affect our expressions of gratitude to the Father. No matter what happened in Jesus' life, He always turned to His Father with a thankful heart. Jesus lived to show us an example of thankfulness. Whatever we do, we do in the name of the Lord Jesus, giving thanks to God through Him.

Colossians 3:17 puts it beautifully: "And whatever you do in word or deed, do all in the name of the Lord Jesus, giving thanks to God and the Father by Him." We can do nothing in our own strength. When we commit our ways to the Lord, He brings them to fruition for our good. That alone calls for thanksgiving. Thanksgiving is a sacrifice we willingly offer to God. Psalm 116:17 says, "I will offer to thee the sacrifice of thanksgiving and will call upon the name of the Lord." It is a sacrifice that flows from His grace, kindness, and longsuffering.

Abuse, humiliation, mocking, persecution—even the threat of death—did not stop Jesus from being thankful to His Father.

Psalm 34:18-19 reassures us: "The Lord is nigh unto them that are of a broken heart and saves such as be of a contrite spirit. Many are the afflictions of the righteous, but the Lord delivers him out of them all." Knowing this empowers us to endure and remain grateful through it all.

Thanks to God's grace, Jesus triumphed over His enemies, death, hell, and the grave. He gave God praise through it all, and we have that same victory by the grace of God. So let us tell God thank you.

5. Truly Care for Others

Galatians 5:14 tells us, "For the entire law is fulfilled in this one command: Love your neighbor as yourself." Only by the grace of God can we truly do this. Grace has to be effective; that is the real test of grace. Do I genuinely care about others?

When we live in grace, we become more like our Lord Jesus. We truly care about others, considering their needs above our own. We're not fake or phony, nor are we chasing after recognition or accolades.

With God's grace working in us, we gain the power to:

- Truly care about others
- Seek ways to build relationships
- Share Christ
- Leave judgment to God
- Keep ourselves from sin and evil

By God's grace through Jesus Christ, we reach out to both saints and sinners. We share Jesus with others in times of joy and sorrow, with no limitations on our outreach—man, woman, boy, or girl, regardless of race or economic status. Everybody needs Jesus in their lives, and we care enough to share Him, letting them know that by grace, they are saved.

Father, thank You for Your grace. Thank You for giving me love, mercy, power, strength, forgiveness, life, and so much more. Because You are gracious to me, I strive to be gracious to others. In Jesus' name, Amen.

Chapter Six

MERCY

Psalm 103:8 reminds us, "The Lord is merciful and gracious, slow to anger and abounding in steadfast love."

Let us be honest: we're all sinners. We have not lived up to who God created us to be. We deserve serious consequences, even the death penalty. But thanks be to God for His incredible mercy. His mercy means He took the pain and suffering for our sins upon Himself. That, my friends, is true mercy.

We are born with the nature of Adam, destined for hell without God's mercy. That is why we recognize that mercy is exactly what we need. Without it, our sentence is death. But, because of God's amazing grace, His mercy stepped in and rescued us from that fate. God could have exacted punishment on Adam right there in the garden when he sinned, but He did not. That is mercy.

In Genesis 3, we see God clothing Adam and sending him out of the garden.

Now Adam was left to navigate a world filled with his own sinful nature.

If we are in Christ, His loving-kindness shields us from the punishment we rightly deserve. Sin and disobedience lead to death. Adam could have faced a much harsher penalty, but it was God's Old Testament mercy that was extended to him. And here is the good news: God is the same yesterday, today, and forever; His mercy still exists.

Psalm 103:10 tells us, "He hath not dealt with us after our sins; nor rewarded us according to our iniquities." He does not punish us as we deserve or repay us according to our wrongs. Just as the sky is high above the earth, so great is His love for those who honor Him. That is mercy. To honor Him is to obey Him and live according to His ways. His will is to show us pity when we stray.

Mercy is not getting what we deserve. It is the result of sincere love and care from God. For all who believe, Jesus has removed the penalty of both spiritual and physical death. Romans 6:23 says, "For the wages of sin is death, but the gift of God is eternal life through Jesus Christ, our Lord." That is mercy—God removing our sin debt and granting us eternal life.

Mercy has a name, and that name is Jesus. Out of His compassion for us, God sent Jesus to shed His blood. This is the essence of God's forgiveness. Jesus had us on His heart when He went to the cross, knowing we were offenders. Instead of condemning us, God chose to save us. The blood of Jesus redeemed us from sin and death.

Romans 3:23 states, "For all have sinned and come short of the glory of God." "All" means no exceptions. We all need the Lord's mercy. We should be grateful for not receiving the sentence we deserve—That is mercy.

Everyone, without exception, has fallen short of God's expectations, His guidelines, His commandments. We have not met His standards. Isaiah 53:5 reminds us, "But He was wounded for our transgressions; He was bruised for our iniquities. The chastisement of our peace was upon Him, and with His stripes, we are healed." This is mercy, and it is happening now. Jesus is alive, and His mercy is active and alive. He does not have to do this again; it is finished. He bore the sins He did not commit. Jesus was despised and rejected, a man of sorrows, acquainted with grief, so that we could be delivered. The Lord God bruised Him to demonstrate the depth of His mercy.

What about us, beloved? Can we endure being despised and rejected? Can we turn the other cheek? Can we bear one another's burdens in prayer and intercession? Can we resist slander, retaliation, and hostility with mercy? Do we respond with anger and revenge? We are called to show mercy as Christ did for us.

Psalm 147:3 tells us, "He healeth the broken in heart and bindeth up their wounds." Because of His mercy, He continues to heal the sick and broken. In John 8:1-11, we read about the woman caught in adultery. There was no denying her guilt. Jesus, embodying the spirit of mercy, reminded everyone present that they, too, were guilty. He said, "Let anyone of you who is without sin be the first to throw a stone at her." Then He told her He did not condemn her and urged her to leave her life of sin. That is mercy.

We do not condone sin and disobedience in our lives, our families, or our friends. But just as Christ forgave us through His mercy, so must we forgive others. You and I face wounds of the spirit—rejection, abandonment, humiliation, betrayal, and injustice. Jesus died for all of that. Because of His indwelling mercy, we can overcome. He was wounded for our sake and delivers us from it all.

So, let us embrace mercy, share it, and live it out in our lives.

Mercy takes away the sting of death. Death, after all, is separation from God. It is the poisonous grip that Satan has on us. That is why Jesus died. He rose to free us from the sting, the hold, that sin had given Satan over our lives. We cannot approach God in a sinful state—we need a Savior. And that Savior is Jesus. He snatches us away from the wrath, the anger, and the fury of God.

As it says in 1 Corinthians 15:55-58, "O death, where is thy sting? O grave, where is thy victory? The sting of death is sin, and the strength of sin is the law. But thanks be to God, which giveth us the victory through our Lord Jesus Christ. Therefore, my beloved brethren, be ye steadfast, unmovable, always abounding in the work of the Lord, for as much as you know that your labor is not in vain in the Lord." The sting—this separation from God caused by sin—has been removed by the blood of Jesus Christ.

Mercy, grace, forgiveness, and victory all have one name: Jesus. Isaiah 53:12 tells us, "Therefore will I divide Him a portion with the great, and He shall divide the spoil with the strong, because He has poured out His soul unto death; and He was numbered with the transgressors, and He bare the sin of many and made intercession for the transgressors." Isaiah 53:5 adds that He was wounded, bruised, and chastised for our sins, and with His stripes, we are healed. 1 Peter 2:24 states, "Who His own self bare our sins in His own body on the tree, that we, being dead to sins, should live unto righteousness; by whose stripes ye were healed." Notice the word "were"—not "going to be" healed. We are healed. That is God's mercy.

Mercy means that God, through Jesus, took the sin and the sting of death—this separation from Him—off of us. Mercy means He took it upon Himself. Grace means He did it all because He loves us.

Jesus sees us today, and His mercy is renewed every day. In the world we live in, we absolutely need God's mercy. We face countless challenges, temptations, tests, and trials. We need mercy! We need grace! Both empower us to witness the salvation of our God. We cannot fix things on our own. Our Lord's mercy keeps us from giving up. We stand firm in the grace (or power) of God. There is no giving up here. Jesus did not give up, and neither will we.

As Lamentations 3:22-25 reminds us, "It is of the Lord's mercies that we are not consumed, because His compassions fail not. They are new every morning; great is Thy faithfulness. The Lord is my portion, saith my soul; therefore, will I hope in Him. The Lord is good unto them that wait for Him, to the soul that seeketh Him."

We are not consumed or destroyed because God keeps us every day. When we face challenges, tests, trials, and suffering, He is faithful to bring us through. He is faithful to have mercy and compassion on us. Great is His faithfulness!

So let us make our affirmation and declaration:

1) I will hope in the Lord. 2) The Lord is my portion (all that I need). 3) The Lord is good to me as I serve Him. 4) My soul seeks after my God, and He is good to me. Amen!

Is there ever a time when we can step outside of God's mercy? Is God always merciful? The answer to both questions is yes. As Romans 9:15 says, "For He said to Moses, I will have mercy, and I will have compassion on whom I will have compassion." God responds to us based on our obedience and submission to Him.

Sin, disobedience, lawlessness, unfaithfulness, and a lack of love and compassion can all put us in a position where we seem exempt from God's mercy. Let us dig a little deeper into this. For instance, in Exodus chapters 7 through 12, Pharaoh had ten chances to submit to and obey God's authority. He turned down each one. In doing so, he rejected mercy and instead chose to face the consequences of the plagues. When we ignore God's mercy by challenging Him, we invite His wrath. Pharaoh refused to honor the one true and living God; he hardened his heart against Him, served idols, and ultimately opted for destruction. I encourage you to read through Exodus chapters 7-12 to see this unfold.

Our challenge is to cast off ignorance and disobedience. God desires to show us His grace, mercy, and power. When our hearts harden, God deals with us accordingly.

Romans 9:18 states, "Therefore hath He mercy on whom He will have mercy, and whom He will He hardeneth." God knows our hearts. When we exhibit strong, willful disobedience, we challenge His mercy, and He responds to our stubbornness and hard-headedness.

So, let us commit to guarding our relationship with our Father.

We need to align ourselves with His will and always desire what He desires. This alignment is crucial for walking in Divine mercy. We do not deserve it, and we cannot buy it, but we can humble ourselves and choose obedience. We can express gratitude for everything He does for us, as He certainly does not have to. Being humble and obedient positions us for God's great mercy.

Father, thank You for Your mercy. I'm grateful that You do not punish me according to what I truly deserve. Help me to extend that same mercy to others. Amen.

Chapter Seven

GLORY

Exodus 33:18-22 tells us about a powerful moment when Moses spoke to God, saying, "Please show me your glory." God responded, saying, "I will make all of my goodness pass before you and I will proclaim before you my name, The Lord. And I will be gracious to whom I will be gracious and will show mercy on whom I will show mercy."

Today, I find myself crying out, "Lord, show me your glory." What was it that Moses truly wanted? He yearned to see God—Yah, the maker, the creator, the life-giver, the provider, the deliverer, the redeemer. Moses longed to know, deep down in his soul, who the Lord really was. And honestly, we're not so different today. Many of us think we know Him well. Sure, we have knowledge and some revelation about Him, but there is so much more to discover. We crave more.

Glory is at the core of who God is.

It embodies His essence, His character, His power, and His reputation. Glory is evident in God's demonstrations, His habitation, and His regulations. Everything He does is for His glory, for His reputation, and for His power.

Like Moses, we often reach a point in our lives where we need to see that glory. Our God is not some distant figure; He is ever-present. He makes this known through His presence, His manifested glory, and His mighty works.

God's glory is encapsulated in His name. In Exodus 3:19, He boldly announces His name and reveals its meaning: "I will be what I will be." "I AM," YHWH. "I AM that I AM, and I do what I want to do." God does not need anyone's permission. He declares that His actions speak for Him. "I do what no one else can do because it is mine... I made it... all of it, and it speaks of My glory," says the Lord.

The created cannot boast about itself. We have no reason to take pride in anything; instead, we glorify our Creator. Psalm 91:1 states, "The heavens declare the glory of God." And in Psalm 24:1-2, we read, "The earth is the Lord's and everything in it, the world and all who live in it; for He founded it on the seas and established it on the waters." That is glory—something no one else could accomplish. Glory is about honor and respect. God deserves the highest honor and the utmost respect. Everything belongs to Him, and He manages it according to His perfect plan. For that, we are truly thankful.

Because He shows us His glory, we have confidence and trust in Him. He reveals Himself through His mighty acts, which are too numerous to list. But here are a few: He separated the waters from the land, created man, flung the sun, moon, and stars into the heavens, parted the seas, was born as a man, died as a man, rose from the dead, saved mankind, performed miracles, and will return in splendor and glory!

If you are reading this right now and going through a tough time, know that the weight of your struggles can sometimes block the glory. The Spirit of the Lord wants you to understand that God's glory is heavier than any burden, bigger than any problem, and more powerful than any crisis or devastation. Here's a suggestion: with a sincere heart, ask God to show you His glory. Tell Him, just as Moses did, "I want to see You." He is the Helper.

He decides how He wants to reveal His glory.

It is not always through natural occurrences, but it certainly can be. He speaks of Himself within us through the Holy Spirit. He is our Helper.

The concept of "Helper" is an essential part of His glory. His reputation is built upon being there when we need Him. Psalm 46:1 tells us, "God is our refuge and strength, a very present help in trouble." He is always there for us! He is our refuge, our safe place. Let us abide there—it is glorious!

Take this personally. Stop trying to figure everything else out and everyone else's issues. Pursue God's glory. He will not withhold Himself from anyone who seeks Him. Jesus sought after His Father's glory just as Moses did. God made Jesus a body, and He became like us—without sin.

In John 17:1-5, Jesus prays, "Father, the hour is come; glorify Thy Son, that the Son also may glorify Thee. As Thou hast given Him power over all flesh, that He should give eternal life to as many as Thou hast given Him. And this is life eternal, that they might know Thee, the only true God, and Jesus Christ whom Thou hast sent. I have glorified Thee on the earth. I have finished the work which Thou gavest me to do; and now, O Father, glorify Thou me with Thine own self, with the glory which I had with Thee before the world was."

Jesus was essentially saying, "Show Yourself powerful, Father. Bring honor to Yourself through me." How could a humiliating death bring God glory? Because God always has a plan to reveal His power. Jesus rose from the dead with all power in His hands—That is how God received the glory. Jesus was obedient unto death because He knew His Father would deliver Him. That is glory.

The suffering we experience in this present age is nothing compared to the glory that shall be revealed. Just as Jesus and His disciples understood this and endured, so can we. Jesus and the disciples focused on the glory of God that was always before them. We also look ahead to the glory that will be revealed. God has a plan—let us work with Him.

As Romans 8:18 says, "For I reckon that the sufferings of this present time are not worthy to be compared with the glory which shall be revealed in us."

We are always in His glory, and there is always more glory to be revealed.

Remember, when God blesses us, it is for His glory. Blessings are like glory bombs!

We have to yield to the glory of God. In Exodus 33, the Lord God told Moses that He would pass before him, but He wouldn't let Moses see Him fully. Instead, God placed Moses in the cleft of a rock and covered him with His hand. When He removed His hand, Moses could see God's back but not His face. At that moment, if Moses had looked upon God's face, he would have fallen dead. God showed Moses grace and mercy by speaking with him, allowing him to see the glory and live to tell about it.

Beloved, today, because of the shed blood of Jesus, we can behold Him face-to-face. There is a glory, a presence, reserved for when we go to be with Him. When we are saved, sanctified, and filled with the Holy Spirit, we get to see Him. John 1:14 tells us, "The Word became flesh and took up residence among us. We saw His glory, the glory of the one and only begotten, full of grace and truth." Glory, grace, mercy, and truth are all packaged in one—Jesus.

God is not hiding; He is revealing Himself. In the Old Covenant, we see God showing Himself and His glory in types and shadows. The tabernacle was a shadow of things to come, the place where

God manifested Himself in that day. Back then, only the high priest could enter the cloud of glory, and if anyone else dared to enter, they would die. Why did God set it up like that?

It was the schoolmaster. God was teaching us that we cannot approach Him any kind of way. His glory is so powerful and so holy that we would perish if we were unworthy. The Lord Jesus had to come and die to change everything. The old tabernacle had to come down, and a new tabernacle had to be erected. Jesus Christ is the new tabernacle, taking up residence by the Holy Spirit in believers. Thus, the glory of God dwells in our temple when we receive Jesus as our Savior.

It is amazing that we become priests and our bodies turn into tabernacles? It is incredible that glory dwells in us as believers! 1 Corinthians 3:16-17 reminds us, "Know ye not that ye are the temple of God and that the Holy Spirit of God dwells in you? If any man defiles the temple of God, him shall God destroy; for the temple of God is holy, which temple ye are."

We are here to showcase our God—not out of pride, but so others can see His glory and desire to know Him. We defile, pollute, and contaminate God's temple when we disgrace His glory.

Just as YAH led His people through the wilderness with a cloud and fire, He is leading us today. We will not wander around aimlessly; the Lord Jesus Christ has given us a more sure path. Jesus is our pillar of cloud and fire—our leader, provider, and protector. He is extraordinary, supernatural, and gracious!

God's reputation is on the line with us. When we realize that we are God's manifested glory—His visible glory—we become powerful. God in us is our hope of glory. As Colossians 1:27 states, "God has chosen to make known among the Gentiles the glorious riches of this mystery, which is Christ in you, the hope of glory."

God's glory changes us, revolutionizes us, and transforms us. We become extraordinary, just like Him. We showcase Him; we put Him on blast for all to see. As 2 Corinthians 3:18 says, "And we all, with unveiled faces, contemplate the Lord's glory, are being transformed into His image with ever-increasing glory, which comes from the Lord, who is the Spirit."

The only covering we need is the blood of the Lord Jesus Christ. His blood has transformed us, changing us into His image. Every day, we walk in God's glory through Christ Jesus. YAH reveals more of His glory to us daily. It will take an eternity to show us all of Himself, which is why we go from glory to glory each day. Each day brings new revelations and understanding of God's glory, made possible through Jesus and the Holy Spirit. Christ working in us makes our ever-increasing efforts fruitful. We become living testimonies of the glory of God.

Colossians 1:26-28 tells us, "Even the mystery which has been hidden from ages and from generations, but now is made manifest to His saints; to whom God would make known what are the riches of the glory of this mystery among the Gentiles, which is Christ in you, the hope of glory; whom we preach, warning every man and teaching every man in all wisdom, that we may present every man perfect in Christ Jesus." We are the saints. Believers in the Lord Jesus are set apart from the world. We become glory bearers.

Glory is rich, plentiful, abundant, deep, prosperous, great, huge, and inexhaustible. Grace adds no sorrow because it represents God's reputation, His power, and His strength. It is also His presence, and it adds absolutely no sorrow. Our glorious Lord changes us from sounding brass and tinkling cymbals—pitiful noise-makers and whiners—into vessels of power, love, grace, and victory. Let the glory of the Lord rise within us!

Isaiah 60:1 proclaims, "Arise, shine, for your light has come, and the glory of the Lord rises upon you." Every day, we rise in God's glory!

Father, thank You for revealing Yourself to me. Thank You for allowing me to see Your greatness, glory, and power. I will be an example of Your reputation on this earth so that men, women, boys, and girls will be drawn to You. Amen.

Chapter Eight

TRUTH

John 8:31-32 tells us that Jesus said to the Jews who believed in Him, "If you continue in my word, you are truly my disciples, and you will know the truth, and the truth will make you free."

In John 14:6, Jesus declares, "I AM the Way, the Truth, and the Life. No man comes to the Father but by me."

These verses leave no room for any definition of truth outside of Jesus. He is the answer to the age-old question: What is truth? Pilate, the Roman ruler who questioned Jesus at His trial, asked boldly, "What is truth?" as recorded in John 18:38. After asking this, he went out again to the Jews and said, "I find in Him no fault at all."

Many today are blind, just like Pilate was. But we are not blind like Pilate. Truth was standing right before him, yet he couldn't see it. Pilate chose to walk in ignorance and unbelief. The Lord of glory was right in front of him, but Pilate was spiritually dead and unable to recognize the truth. From the beginning, humanity has preferred lies. In Genesis 3, Satan told Eve that if she ate from the tree, she would not die, which directly contradicted what God had said. That is how we recognize a lie: it goes against God's word. Lies have their roots in the heart of man. Satan tempts us with lies, and people believe them with their hearts.

In Genesis 3:1-5, we read, "Now the serpent was more subtle than any beast of the field which the Lord God had made. And he said unto the woman, 'Yea, hath God said, Ye shall not eat of every tree of the garden?' And the woman said unto the serpent, 'We may eat the fruit of the trees of the garden; but of the fruit of the tree which is in the midst of the garden, God hath said, Ye shall not eat of it, neither shall ye touch it, lest ye die.' And the serpent said unto the woman, 'Ye shall not surely die. For God doth know that in the day ye eat thereof, then your eyes shall be opened, and ye shall be as gods, knowing good and evil.'"

The rest of the story is quite clear: humanity chose evil. Evil is the root of lies, and Satan is the father of lies. Eve even misrepresented God when she said that God forbade them to touch the tree—an exaggeration of the truth. God only said not to eat from it.

The world is filled with exaggeration and deception. The god of this world, Satan, is the father of lies, and there is no truth in him. As stated in John 8:44, "You are of your father, the devil, and the lusts of your father you will do. He was a murderer from the beginning and abode not in the truth, because there is no truth in him; when he speaks a lie, he speaks of his own, for he is a liar and the father of it."

Satan has been a liar from the very start, and so has mankind. Both Satan and humanity are drawn to lies, favoring what contradicts the word of God. Satan knows better; his goal is to deceive us so that we might miss God's salvation. This is serious. We must love the truth, cherish the truth, and live the truth. And truth has a name: Jesus!

Revelation 21:8 warns us, "But the fearful, and unbelieving, and the abominable, and murderers, and whoremongers, and sorcerers, and idolators, and all liars shall have their part in the lake which burneth with fire and brimstone, which is the second death." That is where Satan wants us to end up—in a place that burns but does not consume; it just keeps burning. Yes, that is the truth.

The opposite of truth is a lie. Jesus came to expose those lies. The enemy of humanity, Satan, keeps people in darkness, loving deception, deceiving others, and being deceived themselves. Those who lie and doubt are children of the devil. Jesus tells us, "You shall know the truth, and the truth will make you free."

Let us take a moment to examine what freedom really means. Freedom is liberation from slavery. It is liberation from the power of someone else. It means being exempt or released from any kind of restraint. Freedom signifies the absence of coercion. In short, freedom means no constraints holding you back. Believers in the Lord Jesus Christ are free. Through His death, burial, and resurrection, Jesus liberated believers from the slavery and power of Satan, evil, and sin. He frees us from the restraints of the world. Unlike the forces of this world, Jesus does not use coercion or constraint; He releases us from the grip of our enemy. Jesus offers us eternal life and victory over death, hell, and the grave. That is the truth! That is Jesus!

As it says in John 8:36, "If the Son therefore shall make you free, ye shall be free indeed." The word "indeed" means you will have confirmation. You will know you are free. And trust me, we will know!

This is not about someday being free; this is about already being free today. Our confirmation does not depend on you or me; it rests solely on Jesus. He has already accomplished our deliverance. We are already free! Free from what? Free from every weight, burden, and sin that torments us. Freedom in Jesus feels amazing—and it truly is amazing. Oh, taste and see that the Lord is good!

Truth and light go hand in hand. When we know the truth, we walk in the light. Jesus is that light, exposing our ugly, sinful nature and revealing the lies of Satan. He shines a light on the hidden things that so easily ensnare us. The truth dwells in the light. As John 3:19 reminds us, "And this is the condemnation: that light has come into the world, and men loved darkness rather than light because their deeds are evil."

Some of us struggle to accept that our deeds can be evil. Some of us have a hard time admitting that we prefer darkness over light. But the truth is, Jesus came to pull us out of that darkness. When we put our faith in the Lord Jesus, we become light ourselves. When something is in the light, it is exposed, seen, and revealed.

When we confess our sins, Jesus shines a light on them, covers them with His blood, and removes the darkness. We become children of the light. As 1 John 1:9 states, "If we confess our sins, He is faithful and just to forgive us our sins and to cleanse us from all unrighteousness. If we say that we have not sinned, we make Him a liar, and His Word is not in us." God cannot lie. So we confess, we believe, and we are forgiven. That is truth.

The truth is that Jesus brings light out of darkness. When we receive this free gift, so much becomes crystal clear. We're not like Pilate, as we read about in John chapters 18 and 19. Pilate refused and rejected the truth; he could not walk in the light. Persuaded by the lies against Jesus, he led Him to the slaughter, sentencing Him to death. Truth and light eluded Pilate's heart. Today, there are thousands who agree with Pilate. Lies about Jesus continue to spread. But we do not believe those lies; we know the truth.

Jesus is right here with us now. The truth and light are in front of us. So, what will we do with Jesus? He has already set us free. That is the truth. Satan comes with deceit and lying wonders, and those deceptions are very real. The Word of God calls them lying wonders, and people perish because they do not embrace the truth. As John 3:19-21 puts it, "And this is the condemnation: that light has come into the world, and men loved darkness rather than light because their deeds are evil. For everyone who does evil hates the light and does not come to the light, lest his deeds should be exposed. But he who does the truth comes to the light, so that his deeds may be made manifest that they are wrought in God." Sadly, people still choose lies over the truth and darkness over light.

John 16:13 reminds us, "Howbeit when He, the Spirit of Truth is come, He will guide you into all truth: for He shall not speak of Himself; but whatsoever He shall hear, that shall He speak; and He will show you things to come." Jesus is the Spirit of Truth, receiving wisdom from the Father and revealing it to us. He unveils the past, present, and future. Because of His obedience in dying on the cross and rising again, He is crowned the King of All.

The Holy Spirit could not come without the resurrection of Jesus Christ. The truth is that Jesus entered the world to save sinners.

During His time on earth, Jesus embodied truth. His very presence confirmed that God sent Him, evident through His power, love, and authority.

He demonstrated power over nature, demons, sickness, disease, death, and earthly authorities. He is God incarnate, capable of speaking and creating. Nothing we encounter is too complex for Him.

To truly know who He is, we must spend time in the Word of God. The Scriptures reveal our identity as bearers of truth and light. Jesus is The Word. To grasp the essence of Jesus and truth, we need to saturate ourselves in the Word of God—morning, afternoon, evening, and throughout the night. In the Word, we discover what God says, who He is, and what He desires for us. With the Holy Spirit within us, we hear His voice, recall His miracles, and know that He remains the miracle worker. The truth is that He can do anything.

The essence of truth is this: the Word of God is Jesus. John 1:1 declares, "In the beginning was the Word, and the Word was with God, and the Word was God." God's Word—Jesus—within us empowers us to walk as He did. Jesus instructed His disciples in Matthew 10:8, "Heal the sick, cleanse the lepers, raise the dead, cast out devils: freely you have received, freely give." When we embrace the truth, we can live it out. So, why aren't we doing these things? Could it be that we doubt our ability? Have the lies of doubt and unbelief about who Jesus is taken root in our hearts?

Let us be honest: as disciples of Christ, we have work to do and assignments to fulfill. The enemy, Satan—the ultimate liar—wants us to believe we have no authority. That is a falsehood. He wants us to doubt our ability to live out Matthew 10:8.

Moreover, the enemy will even taint the truth with deceptive wonders and false prophets. There are charlatans among us who exploit the faith for their own gain, twisting God's Word for selfish purposes. Without the Holy Spirit, discerning these individuals can be challenging.

1 Timothy 3:8 warns deacons, but it applies to the entire body of Christ: we must not be double-tongued (liars), not given to wine (drunkards), and not driven by the love of money for selfish gain. The truth is that money itself is not evil; it is the misuse of it that corrupts.

God calls us to be honest. Dishonesty leads to deception and evil ways. Walking in truth allows us to expose lies and deceit. Knowing Jesus protects us from falsehood. Remember, we know the truth—Jesus—and He has set us free.

Our prayer is to continue walking in truth and becoming stronger disciples. We aspire to be doers of the Word. Acting on the Word will draw people to Jesus and reveal the truth of God's kingdom. We know who we are, and we know whose we are!

Ultimately, living a life rooted in truth requires us to separate from worldly ways. This journey must be empowered by the Holy Spirit, who helps us set aside the common human tendency to lie. We need Him to help us combat falsehoods, recognize deceivers, and expose lies. We know the Truth. The truth is Jesus, and we are free indeed!

Father, thank You for the Spirit of Truth dwelling within me. Thank You for Jesus, the light of truth shining in my life. There is no bondage or deceit in me because Jesus lives in me. I believe Ephesians 4:21—I have heard, believed, and been taught that the truth is in Jesus. Amen.

Chapter Nine

POWER

Job 26:7-14 says, "God stretches the northern sky over empty space and hangs the earth on nothing. He wraps rain in thick clouds, and the clouds do not burst under their weight. He covers the face of the moon, shrouding it with His clouds. He created the horizon when He separated the waters, setting the boundary between day and night. The foundations of heaven tremble; they shudder at His rebuke. By His power, the sea grew calm. By His skill, He crushed the great sea monster. His Spirit made the heavens beautiful, and His power pierced the gliding serpent. These are just the beginning of all that He does—merely a whisper of His power. Who then can comprehend the thunder of His power?"

Now that is power! Do you know anyone who can do these things? Even just one of them?

To me, power means the ability to do whatever it is you want to do. But how does the dictionary define power?

Power is the ability to act or produce an effect. It is the possession of authority over others. It also means authority, control, dominion, strength, might, force, and ability. There are levels of power:

- Man is given power by God to live and thrive.
- Satan has power because he was created with it, but his power is permissive and limited. He can only act within the boundaries set by God.
- Our power comes from God, and we can use it however we wish.

Thinking and making decisions is a form of power.

Satan can use his limited power, but his intentions are to kill, steal, and destroy. Why? Because God, who has all power, allows it. However, God also gives us the power to defeat Satan. Satan's power is limited compared to God, who has unlimited power. Our God-given power is greater than Satan's because our God is the greatest. Greater is He who is in us (the Lord) than he who is in the world (Satan).

Everything is subject to the power of God. He is all-powerful, full of might, and we know Him as Almighty. That means we can try to contend with Him, but the Almighty always wins.

As Job 40:2 reminds us, the Lord asked Job, "Shall a fault-finder contend with the Almighty?" To contend means to struggle to overcome or overpower. We might try to resist God, but the Almighty will prevail. His power cannot be defeated. Job 26:7-14 outlines God's power and His mighty acts. Power is demonstrated in our homes; when the power is on, it is shown through illumination. The light overcomes darkness. This is why 1 John 1:1-5 states, "And the earth was without form and void, and darkness was upon the face of the deep." This chaos is referred to as Tohu va Bohu. God brings order, light, and power to that chaos and darkness.

1 John 1:5 says, "God is light, and in Him is no darkness at all." When He dwells in us, He brings power. He shines His light on whatever challenges we face, helping us overcome them. Genesis 1:3 states, "And God said, 'Let there be light,' and there was light." That is the power and light that dwell in us through Jesus. God is the source of light and life—no room for debate there.

The creation account in Genesis Chapters 1 and 2 clearly declares the power of God. You and I are a result of His power. Without Him, nothing was made that is made. Genesis 2:7 tells us, "And the

Lord God formed man of the dust of the ground and breathed into his nostrils the breath of life, and man became a living soul."

Breathing life into a structure made of dirt is pure power. AI cannot compare to that level of creation. Everything man creates comes from something that already exists. God starts with nothing and makes something. There is truly no better word for it than power.

So here we are today, breathing the breath of God. It is not our breath; every soul is alive because of God's breath within us. We make choices: we can either love and obey God, who gives us the power to live, or we can love and obey Satan, who comes to steal, kill, and destroy.

God gave us the power to choose between life and death. In Deuteronomy 30:19, it says, "Today I have given you a choice between life and death, between blessings and curses. Now I call on heaven and earth to witness the choice you make. Oh, that you would choose life so that you and your descendants might live!"

We truly have the power of choice. If God is your choice, then serve Him; if Satan is your choice, then serve him.

But remember, the consequences of serving Satan are severe and detrimental. Man was created in God's image, with the power to be like Him, but instead, man chose to align with Satan. God infused His own DNA into humanity, yet through Adam, that seed was contaminated by evil. So, the Lord God made a way for us to be born again, and it is nothing short of miraculous. We do not go back into our mother's womb; instead, through God's power and His ability to do what only He can do, He transforms us into new creatures.

This new creature walks in power and light. As it says in 1 Peter 2:9, "But you are a chosen generation, a royal priesthood, a holy nation; a peculiar people that you should show forth the praises of Him who hath called you out of darkness into His marvelous light."

Only God can take our old, sinful, dark nature and transform it into something beautiful, powerful, and acceptable to Him. Believers are chosen, royal, and holy because of the power of God dwelling within them.

It takes God's power to bring about change in us. When we change, God promises to change our descendants as well.

Change means stepping away from one thing and moving toward another. We take off the old man and put on the new.

This new creature is powerful. Remember Job 26:7-14? That is the very power we have living inside us. Because of the blood of the Lord Jesus Christ, we have become new creatures in Christ Jesus.

In Luke 10:19, it states, "Behold, I give unto you power to tread on serpents and scorpions, and over all the power of the enemy: and nothing shall by any means hurt you." To "tread" means to trample, to cross over something, or to dominate and destroy it. This passage shows Christ giving us the authority to stomp on the enemy. He empowers us to advance into the enemy's territory with authority, strength, and confidence.

Serpents and scorpions represent the deadly attacks of the devil. These attacks aim to make us fearful and stagnant. This is where the power of God within us defeats the enemy.

The serpents and scorpions refer to demons, evil spirits, and everything connected with Satan. These verses encompass all of Satan's power linked to the serpent, as seen in Genesis 3:14-15.

In the Bible, scorpions symbolize sickness, death, and demonic oppression. They can also represent terror, torment, and punishment. But God has given us power and authority over all of this. This power is not based on feelings or emotions; it is grounded in the Word of God. We must understand that it is God's power working through us.

Luke 10:19 assures us that nothing shall harm or hurt you. "Nothing" means not anything, no thing. God, through the Lord Jesus Christ, destroys the works of the enemy. All of the enemy's works are rendered void, blank, and without substance. We need the Holy Spirit to reveal this truth to us. Nothing will harm us because of the power of God within us. We are new creatures. We are not mere putty in Satan's hands; we are born again. The power that was lost in the Garden of Eden has been restored to us by the blood of the Lord Jesus Christ.

Acts 1:8 says, "But ye shall receive power, after that the Holy Ghost has come upon you. And ye shall be witnesses unto me, in Jerusalem and in all Judea, and in Samaria, and unto the uttermost part of the earth."

We are called to let our light—that power—shine for the whole world to see. It is not about us; it is about giving praise to God. This is all for His reputation. People see us, but they should be giving Him the props!

Father God, I choose life and the light that comes through Jesus Christ. Thank You for the power of Your Holy Spirit dwelling within me. Amen.

Chapter Ten

FAITH

Hebrews 11:1 says, "Now faith is the substance of things hoped for, and the evidence of things not seen."

Hebrews 11:5 adds, "But without faith, it is impossible to please God: for He that comes to God must believe that He is, and that He is a rewarder of them that diligently seek Him."

This is an important word that relates to our Christian walk. We know what faith means to us, but it can be tough to explain it to others. So, I'm going to share how I see faith and how it operates in my life. I pray this helps anyone who reads it.

Faith is now. "Now" means at the present moment, at this time, at once, immediately. It captures the situation with things as they are.

Those of us with children really understand what "now" means. We do not need to teach them the concept; they just get it. Whatever they want, they want it right now!

Ephesians 3:20 says, "Now unto him that is able to do exceeding abundantly above all that we ask or think according to the power that worketh in us." There is that "now" word. Immediately, without hesitation, we give thanks to God. Walking by faith is always immediate. We do not have to wait. Waiting seems to imply the passing of time filled with doubt and hesitation—maybe thinking it might happen, or just watching the clock tick-tock.

For believers in Christ, waiting is active. It is work for us. We wait in prayer, praise, and presence. Waiting is brief for believers because we spend that time expecting, not complaining; praying, not grumbling; and being in His presence, not scatterbrained and doubting.

Whatever God has said in the Old Covenant and the New Covenant is 'now.' Has it occurred in the natural yet? Maybe not, but believers know it is now. "Now" is powerful. Each moment is now. Every minute, month, and year is now. God is working now!

The word that comes after "now" in Hebrews 11:1 is faith. Faith is unquestioning belief. It does not need, nor does it require, evidence or proof. That is the God kind of faith. The first step is to believe that God exists.

The second part is to know that God actually does things. He's not a fairytale or a figment of our imagination—He is real. Faith is knowing Him without seeing. For example, Abraham had faith in what God told him.

Faith is knowing without seeing. The Word of promise was given to Abraham by God. Romans 4:17 states, "(As it is written, I have made thee a Father of many nations,) before Him whom he believed, even God who quickened the dead, and calleth those things which are not as though they were."

We are told further in Romans 4 that Abraham staggered not—he was not shaken by unbelief and doubt. He waited twenty-five years. Year after year, he did not stumble. Did he think about it? Most likely. Did he get ridiculed? Most likely. Year after year, he had hope. To Abraham, each year was 'NOW.' Abraham believed God! Look, beloved, it is not taking too long; it is taking the right number of hours, months, and years for our faith and hope to be manifested.

Abraham waited 25 years. Those years felt like "NOW" to him because he believed God. You see, whatever God says, He means, and no one and nothing can change that—that is faith. At long last, Abraham had the son of promise.

For 25 years, he rejoiced in hope. Every day was 'now' for him. When the 'now' seems to be taking a long time, we continue to hope. Faith is the substance of things hoped for. Faith is the substance of hope.

What is the relationship between faith and hope?

Hope is the anticipation part. This is important: faith is what hope is made of—faith supports hope. Hope keeps us focused on what we're believing for, filled with rejoicing. Because our God 1. answers and provides, 2. never lies, and 3. is faithful, we rejoice and hope. Abraham woke up in hope every day, thinking, "This is the day." The same spirit of hope sustained him through 25 years of faith.

Faith is the substance of hope. Hope is anticipation; it is forward-looking. Faith refuses doubt and rules out stress. Hope is the stress destroyer. Romans 12:12 says, "Rejoicing in hope; patient in tribulation; continuing in prayer." Sometimes, things sound too good to be true or too simple to be effective. But we're to be joyful while we anticipate. We're to see tribulation as strength and stamina builders. Prayer is our stabilizer—it keeps us focused, eliminates worry, and works NOW.

Hebrews 11:1 tells us that faith is evidence. It also states that faith is the evidence of things not seen. If it is not seen, how can I know it is? What is evidence?

Evidence is information or facts that prove something is valid or true. The evidence we have is the Word of God. The Word of God fills us with faith and hope. I'm convinced that if He said it, He meant it, and so shall it be. The Bible is our evidence. God's faithfulness is the proof. We go from faith to faith, increasing in faith daily as we pour God's Word into us. We rejoice in hope daily. This all comes through the evidence that God gives us in His Word.

Let us look at some evidence of faith and hope from the Word of God. In Matthew 8:5-13, a Roman officer approached Jesus about healing his sick, paralyzed servant. The centurion showed 'now' faith as well as rejoicing 'hope' when he came to Jesus. The Roman soldier was a servant of Caesar, the Roman ruler, but hope overruled his loyalty to man. He said to Jesus, "Lord, I do not deserve to have you come under my roof, but just say the word, and my servant will be healed." And so it was. Jesus sent the Word—because Jesus is the Word—and His servant was healed that very hour.

Right here, the Word of God gives us evidence of faith and hope.

Speak the Word. Jesus is the Word. We have the written Word of God as proof or evidence of His power. Jesus is the written Word of God, and He is the manifestation of that Word. His words leap off the pages and do what God says. That is what we, as believers, know.

The woman with the issue of blood in Mark 5:25-34 came up behind Jesus. She said to herself, "If I can just touch the border, the hem, or the bottom part of His garment, I will be made whole." Touching the border of His garment was hope. When she said, "I will be made whole," that was the manifestation of faith. It is 'now' faith. Her faith was 'now.' She knew that the moment she touched Him, she would be healed. I believe there are times when the 'now' is immediate, just like with this woman. At other times, the 'now' is in our hearts. With anticipation and hope, we hold onto the truth that God said it, and so shall it be! Jesus told the woman that her faith had healed her. What about you and me? Let us not give up. We have the evidence in the Word of God.

This woman in Mark chapter 5 was bold. She was desperate. Hope and faith together make us bold.

She moved through that crowd with hope and anticipation, and then her faith assured her that when she touched Jesus, she would be made whole. Jesus honored her faithfulness and said in Mark 5:34, "Daughter, thy faith hath made thee whole; go in peace and be healed of thy plague."

This woman's belief propelled her toward her goal of touching Jesus. Belief is the starting point. It gets you up and moving. Hope energizes you. Faith gets the job done—in Jesus' name.

In Matthew 9:28, we read, "And when He had come into the house, the blind men came to Him; and Jesus said unto them, 'Believe ye that I am able to do this?' They said unto Him, 'Yea, Lord.'" Jesus touched their eyes and told them that it was according to their faith that it happened for them. Their eyes were opened, and when they departed, they spread His fame throughout all that country.

Now they had evidence, and when you have evidence, you become a witness. A witness testifies to what has happened. They were healed by Jesus through the Word of God. They believed He could do it, and He did. And He is still doing His Word today.

Belief is key. It is the key that unlocks miracles. Unbelief cancels faith and smothers hope. Because of unbelief, we miss out on the miracles and victories we can have in Christ Jesus. So let us hold onto our faith and keep believing!

Belief in Christ is the measure of faith. Romans 12:3 says, "For I say through the grace given unto me, to every man that is among you, not to think of himself more highly than he ought to think; but to think soberly, according as God hath dealt to every man the measure of faith." A measure is the correct and appropriate amount; it tells us the extent or limitations. God has given believers the necessary and full amount of faith they need.

Along with the measure of faith comes the measure of grace. "But unto every one of us is given grace according to the measure of the gift of Christ." God's grace is the power to believe His Word. Believing His Word is the evidence of our faith.

In Matthew 17:17, Jesus answered and said, "O faithless and perverse generation; how long shall I be with you? How long shall I suffer you? Bring him hither to me." The disciples struggled to cast out a demonic spirit from a possessed young boy. Jesus knew they were operating in fear and unbelief, and it troubled Him.

Let us not frustrate the grace of God through unbelief. He has given us enough faith to face any situation.

Jesus told the disciples to bring the possessed boy to Him. Jesus is the healer, the Word, the Hope. We do what we do only through Him, and the child was healed. Jesus did it, and He always does. We have 'now' faith!

When Jesus' disciples wondered why they couldn't free the boy, He answered, "Because of your unbelief; for verily, I say unto you, if you have faith as a grain of mustard seed, ye shall say unto this mountain, 'Remove hence to yonder place,' and it shall remove; and nothing shall be impossible unto you. Howbeit, this kind goeth not out, but by prayer and fasting."

Here we see that even if we have little faith, prayer and fasting can build and nourish it. Being built up in Him through prayer and fasting, we become mountain movers.

Mountains can be faith destroyers and hope removers. They attack a believer's confidence in the evidence from God's Word. "Hath God said? Did God mean what He said?"

Mountains can take many forms—sickness, disease, family disorders, generational curses, economic crises, loneliness, harmful habits, and so much more.

Jesus said "nothing shall be impossible" for us. Impossible means something that cannot be done under any circumstances. Our Lord assures us that we can do it. Our God specializes in the impossible becoming possible. He even gives us a guarantee: we can be certain of the outcome. God's Word is our covenant, our bond, our assurance. We have a record of His mighty acts.

Jesus encourages us to start where we are. A mustard seed is tiny but grows into a big, lush plant, and so it is with our faith. We can have great faith through the evidence that God provides in His Word.

Finally, our God is a rewarder. A reward is something given in recognition of one's service, pointing out effort and achievement. God acknowledges our efforts to become more of who He wants us to be. He recognizes us because we believe in Him and rejoices in us because we rejoice in Him and His works. Our God is amazing. He blesses us with benefits or rewards for having faith in Him. He loads us with benefits because we know that He is good.

So, what is the reward He gives to believers? How does He recognize us, and for what achievements? What have we achieved through faith?

Here is my personal list of some of the rewards for those who walk by faith:

- Eternal life
- Joy unspeakable and full of glory
- Power to move mountains
- Overcoming and defeating the devil
- Power to perform miracles
- Being sound—spirit, soul, and body
- Living holy through the Holy Spirit

Father, thank You that I have the measure of faith. I believe Your Word. I believe that Jesus is Your Word working in me. I live by faith in the Son of God, Jesus, the beginning and end of my faith. Amen.

Chapter Eleven

FORGIVENESS

Romans 3:23: "For all have sinned and fall short of the glory of God; and all are justified freely by His grace through the redemption that came by Christ Jesus."

1 John 1:9: "If we confess our sins, He is faithful and just and will forgive us our sins and purify us from all unrighteousness."

Matthew 6:12-15: "And forgive us our debts, as we forgive our debtors. And lead us not into temptation, but deliver us from evil. For thine is the Kingdom, and the power, and the glory forever. Amen. For if you forgive men their trespasses, your heavenly Father will also forgive you; but if you do not forgive men their trespasses, neither will your Father forgive you your trespasses."

The Word of God includes everyone under sin. The Bible says that all have sinned.
When we sin, we do not meet God's expectations; we let Him down. So, everyone needs forgiveness. "Everyone" means no exceptions.

ALL includes every race, creed, and nationality, male and female, regardless of educational or professional status, slave or free! Everybody has sinned. Everybody needs forgiveness.

Every person alive, or who has ever lived, has gone beyond the boundaries God set for our behavior. The Bible explains that because Adam and Eve were disobedient, sin came upon all mankind. Romans 5:12-19 states, "Therefore, just as through one man sin entered the world and death through sin, and thus death spread to all men..."

Adam was given specific instructions from God, but he chose to do otherwise and disobey. Genesis 2:16-17 says, "You may surely eat of every tree of the garden, but of the tree of the knowledge of good and evil, you shall not eat of it; for in the day that you eat thereof, you shall surely die." The Word of God gives clear instructions; our duty is to obey. Adam and Eve are our spiritual parents. They sinned and passed that sinful nature on to all who come after. We need a Savior.

Eve was not formed or made by God until Genesis 2:21-22: "And the Lord God caused a deep sleep to fall upon Adam, and he slept; and He took one of his ribs and closed up the flesh instead thereof. And the rib, which the Lord God had taken from man, made He a woman and brought her unto the man."

Eve had a significant impact on Adam—more impact than God, in a way. Eve had an encounter with Satan. She misquoted the Word of God, and she and Adam disobeyed God's Word and His instructions. They sinned and disregarded God's commands. Adam definitely knew better. Eve was deceived or lied to by Satan.

Genesis 3:1: "Now the serpent was more subtle than any beast of the field which the Lord God had made, and he said unto the woman, 'Yea, hath God said, ye shall not eat of every tree of the garden?'"

This is when the red flag goes up. When God says something, it is exactly what He says, and it is what He means. The enemy of our souls, Satan, wants us to question God's Word. Once we start questioning God's Word, we set ourselves up for disobedience and sin. Satan knows how to plant seeds of disobedience.

When we distort God's Word, it becomes easy to do just as Eve and Adam did. God's instruction was to not eat of the tree, but Eve added that they were not to touch it. She misrepresented God.

She twisted the Word of God, which is a common occurrence today. The end result was that Adam and Eve were expelled from the garden. God does not tolerate sin. Sin and disobedience separate us from God. They were alive in the natural but died spiritually. They had children, from whom we all descend. Because of Adam and Eve's sin, all mankind is born sinful and full of sin. Man distorts the Word of God, changes the truth into lies, and loves evil more than good.

I look at it like this: we all inherited the sin nature from Adam and Eve. Psalm 51:5 says, "Behold, I was brought forth in iniquity, and in sin, my mother conceived me." That is what came through Adam and Eve. We believe we have been delivered from sin and trespass. By the blood of the Lord Jesus Christ, we are forgiven.

It is not God's will that any should perish! And sin causes men to perish. To perish means to wither up, to dry up, to end up somewhere you do not want to go. So, our God forgives us of sin, trespass, iniquity, and transgression. That is why we pray, "forgive us our debts." We owe a debt to God we cannot pay.
Jesus paid the sin debt when He was crucified, died, yet lived! To continue in sin is rebellion against the righteous God.

Trespass is a direct violation of something known to be forbidden. You know what you are doing. It is lawlessness. It is stepping into a wrong place while pretty much knowing better than to go there. Thank God for forgiveness! This is serious because it makes us accountable. We do it even when we know better, even if it is forbidden. Only the blood of Jesus can erase such sin.

Sin is the deliberate and purposeful violation of the will of God. This includes the lust of the flesh, the lust of the eye, and the pride of life. Lust means an overwhelming desire, uncontrollable urges, and even compulsive behavior. It just resounds, "I couldn't help it." Jesus was tempted in all these ways, but He did not sin. He could have sinned, but He did not, so that we could be forgiven by our Father in heaven.

Hebrews 4:14-16 states, "...For our high priest (Jesus) is able to understand our weaknesses. He was tempted in every way we are, but He did not sin."

Hebrews 7:24-26 says, "But this man, because He continues forever, has an unchangeable priesthood. Wherefore, He is able also to save them to the uttermost that come unto God by Him, seeing He ever lives to make intercession for them. For such a high priest became us, who is holy, harmless, undefiled, separate from sinners, and made higher than the heavens." That means Jesus meets all of God's requirements for a sinless, obedient life.

Iniquity is filthy. Iniquity refers to grossly immoral behavior. Immoral means having no standard of what is right. Iniquity carries with it no caution or shame in what one does. It is gross behavior, wickedness. Think of it as doing the unthinkable without remorse.

How can such behavior be forgiven? Murder, adultery, molestation—these are just three examples. It is hard for us to forgive such actions. If we take it personally when it is done to us, how do we think God sees it?

Even with iniquity, if we confess our sin, He is just and forgives. Too often, we abuse the Word of God when we commit sin, knowing that God forgives. That is blatant disrespect for God's sacrifice of His Son, Jesus. We act as if Jesus' blood was not enough.
Transgression is going beyond the limits God sets. Remember, Adam and Eve went too far. They overstepped, crossed over the boundaries that God set for them. "Trans" means to go beyond, and "gression" refers to going beyond

the limit. God has set limits on our behavior, but we transgress. We go beyond the limit. We must be forgiven. Only God can forgive. When He forgives, He cleanses, casts the sin into a sea of forgetfulness, and remembers it no more.

Psalm 103:8-14: "The Lord is merciful and gracious, slow to anger and plenteous in mercy. He will not always chide; neither will He keep His anger forever. He has not dealt with us after our sins, nor rewarded us according to our iniquities. For as the heaven is high above the earth, so great is His mercy toward them that fear Him. As far as the east is from the west, so far hath He removed our transgressions from us. Like a father pitieth his children, so the Lord pitieth them that fear Him. For He knoweth our frame; He remembereth that we are dust."

Forgiveness is necessary. It is not just an option; it is a necessity. Only the Lord Jesus can remove the penalty of sin from us. The Father respects the Son. Micah 7:19 says, "He will again have compassion on us and will subdue our iniquities. You will cast all our sins into the depths of the sea." Every person born into this world needs forgiveness. Jesus is God's forgiveness.

Forgiveness is intentional. God has decided to let go of any resentment or retaliation against us. He forgives our disobedience—that is God's mercy. His requirement is that we confess our sins. When we confess, God purifies us of all unrighteousness. If we are purified, made pure or clean, we are forgiven.

We cannot purify (or clean) ourselves because we are the sinners. Maybe we want to do right, but wrong is ever-present. We need help. And it is the blood of Jesus that cleanses us. Unrighteousness means not right or without right. We need God's Spirit to do right in His sight.

To confess means to admit that you have committed a crime or fault in some way. We are often slow to do that because of shame, embarrassment, or guilt. Although God already knows, He wants us to confess to Him. He asked Adam and Eve, "What have you done?"

Genesis 3:13: "And the Lord said unto the woman, 'What is this that thou hast done?'"
And the woman said, "The serpent beguiled me, and I did eat." Owning up to it is powerful. There was no reason to lie. She knew God knew, and she knew she had sinned. She tried to shift the blame onto Satan. But everyone must bear the burden of their iniquities. That is why EVERYONE must be forgiven by God.

The other part of this is that when He forgives us our trespasses, we are to forgive those who trespass against us. This is the difficult part. What if someone wrongs me, accuses me falsely, or misuses and abuses me in some manner? What am I to do? This might be the hard part for each of us. There are mean-spirited people, and without God's Spirit, they do all sorts of things. Some even claim to have His Spirit but display a serpent-like nature. We are instructed to forgive. God will handle them. Our job is to do the right thing.

Colossians 3:13: "Bear with each other and forgive one another, if any of you has a grievance against someone. Forgive as the Lord forgave you." We can do this only out of deep love and compassion from the Holy Spirit. We do it out of deep respect for God. Our natural self cannot. It is not optional.

How many times must we forgive?
Matthew 18:21-22: Jesus said, "I say not unto thee until seven times; but until seventy times seven." Mercy carries no resentment or anger. The one forgiven might not show any remorse. Our task is to free ourselves from disobeying God.

Forgiveness does not mean condoning. To condone means to agree with, approve of, or show support for. We do not approve of sin in our lives or in others' lives.

Forgiveness does not mean absence of correction. God, through Jesus, does the best correction because He gives perfect love even in punishment. He "will handle it," which encourages us to forgive.

Father, thank You for giving me this opportunity to thank You for forgiveness. I repent of any trespass against You. I repent of any offense to my fellow man. Thank You for Your mercy and loving-kindness. Amen.

Chapter Twelve

SALVATION

Acts 4:12: "Neither is there salvation in any other; for there is none other name under heaven given among men, whereby we must be saved."

Matthew 1:21: "And she shall bring forth a son, and thou shalt call his name Jesus; for He shall save His people from their sins."

Matthew 5:24: Jesus said, "Verily, verily, I say unto you, he that heareth my word and believeth on Him that sent Me hath everlasting life and shall not come into condemnation, but is passed from death to life."

The word salvation means preservation. It is deliverance from harm, ruin, or loss. It means deliverance from sin and the consequences of sin.

Preservation means keeping something valued alive and free from damage or decay.

Deliverance means to be rescued. It means to be set free from bondage. It means to be freed from slavery and to be drawn out.

A savior is one who preserves and delivers. Everyone alive now needs a savior. Everyone who has ever lived needed a savior. Everyone, with no exclusions, needs Jesus Christ.

Only Jesus Christ keeps believers from destruction, decay, and ruin. Jesus is the savior and redeemer.

Redeem means to gain or regain possession of something in exchange for payment. Jesus paid the price of His blood for our sins. That is redemption. That is how we become His.

Galatians 3:22: "But the scripture hath concluded all under sin, that the promise by faith of Jesus Christ might be given to them that believe." We have all sinned, but when we believe in Jesus as our redeemer, we are saved from ruin and destruction.

Galatians 3:13: "Christ hath redeemed us from the curse of the law, being made a curse for us: for it is written, 'Cursed is everyone that hangeth on a tree.'"

This is the reality: Man is sinful. Man was cursed because of sin. There is no way for us to get rid of the sin except through the Lord Jesus Christ.

In chapter 11 of this book on forgiveness, we learned that all have sinned. There are no exceptions. Everybody needs a savior. We cannot save ourselves. Chapter 11 on forgiveness made it clear that we must repent. When we repent, God forgives us of our sins, and He cleanses us of all unrighteousness.

Repent means to confess and forsake. God is calling all men to repent and believe the Gospel of Jesus Christ. The Gospel is the saving message of salvation.

John 3:16: "For God so loved the world, that He gave His only begotten Son, that whosoever believeth in Him should not perish, but have everlasting life."

We have to believe, repent, and receive. Look, you might have a warm pair of socks in a drawer. It is very cold, and your feet are cold. The socks are there for you. Your feet could be warm, but you must get the socks, put them on, and wear them.

So it is with salvation; salvation is always present. Jesus will not be crucified again. It is a finished work. Go to Him, confess, and receive deliverance. This is not something forced on anyone. It only costs surrender.

1 Timothy 1:15-16: "This is a faithful saying, and worthy of all acceptation, that Christ Jesus came into the world to save sinners, of whom I am chief. Howbeit, for this cause, I obtained mercy, that in me first Jesus Christ might show forth all long-suffering, for a pattern to them which should hereafter believe on Him to life everlasting."

Jesus, through God, showed mercy and long-suffering when He was sacrificed for the sins of the world. He did it to save sinners, and such were we. Timothy said of himself that he was the chief of sinners. Well, there is stiff competition between him and me. That is how we come to God: we come knowing that we are sinners. We know that we need a Savior. God is long-suffering, merciful, and not willing that we perish. We believe upon the Lord Jesus Christ, and we are forgiven. We have eternal, everlasting life in Him.

John 3:17-19: "For God sent not His Son into the world to condemn the world; but that the world through Him might be saved. He that believes on Him is not condemned; but he that believes not is condemned already, because he has not believed in the name of the only begotten Son of God. And this is the condemnation, that light has come into the world, and men loved darkness rather than light because their deeds are evil."

Condemnation means to declare guilty. In God's sight, we are all sinners. Yet, in God's sight, we are not guilty when we receive Jesus as our Savior. God delays judgment, giving us time to repent, but we do not frustrate Him by continuing in sin.

2 Peter 3:9: "The Lord knoweth how to deliver the godly out of temptations, and to reserve the unjust unto the day of judgment to be punished." Godly people always thank Him for delivering them out of temptation.

Falling into sin separates us from God. That is why we stay in Christ; for in Christ, there is no condemnation and no separation. If God is for us, who can be against us?

Romans 8:33-34: "Who shall lay anything to the charge of God's elect? It is God that justifieth. Who is he that condemneth?

It is Christ that died, yea, rather, that is risen again, who is even at the right hand of God, who also maketh intercession for us."

Condemnation brings death. God's judgment for sin is death. God decides what happens to the sinner. Only God is the lawgiver, judge, and jury. Those who receive Jesus pass from death to life.

John 10:27-28: "My sheep hear my voice, and I know them, and they follow me. And I give unto them eternal life, and they shall never perish. Neither shall any man pluck them out of my hand."

John 17:1-3: Jesus said, "Father, the hour is come; glorify thy Son, that thy Son also may glorify thee. As thou hast given Him power over all flesh, that He should give eternal life to as many as thou hast given Him. And this is life eternal, that they might know thee, the only true God, and Jesus Christ whom thou hast sent."

Perish means ruin, destruction, rot, decay, and loss. That is man's state without Christ. That is the eternal state without Christ.

Eternal means lasting or existing forever. It means never-ending and continuous.

We have a choice. We can decide between everlasting rot and being lost, or we can choose life with Christ. It is a today—right now—decision.

Jesus told the man on the cross next to Him in Luke 23:43, "Verily I say unto thee, today shalt thou be with me in paradise." Paradise is being in the presence of God. Not being in God's presence is hell. One word for hell is Sheol, the place of suffering.

John 3:36 says, "He that believeth on the Son hath everlasting life: and he that believeth not the Son shall not see life; but the wrath of God abideth on him."

In John 5:24, we read, "Verily, verily, I say unto you, he that heareth my word and believeth on Him that sent me hath everlasting life and shall not come into condemnation: but is passed from death unto life."

Father, in the name of Jesus, Thank you for forgiving me of my sins. Thank you for Jesus, my Savior. I receive eternal life through the redeeming blood of Jesus Christ. Amen.

*To contact the author email:
overseerbetty@gmail.com*

www.ingramcontent.com/pod-product-compliance
Lightning Source LLC
Chambersburg PA
CBHW070548090426
42735CB00013B/3109